The Nutcracker begins at Clara's house on Christmas Eve when a toy nutcracker – made by Clara's godfather, Drosselmeyer – transforms into a prince. Clara and the prince travel to the Land of Sweets, and along the way, they meet gingerbread soldiers, the Mouse King, and the Sugar Plum Fairy herself.
Ballet steps are airy, press to hear the Sugar Plum Fairy!
A dance for two people is called a "pas de deux". Many great ballets include a *pas de deux*.
W0259652

Just like Clara in *The Nutcracker*, Mia and Leo start shrinking until they are small enough to fit inside Mia's dollhouse. "Are we dreaming?" Mia asks. "I'm definitely awake. I think it must be magic!" Leo replies. Just then, Mia's favourite doll finds them. "Hello," the doll says. "My name's Coppélia." Mia and Leo gasp. They've never met a talking doll before! "Maybe we can be friends?" suggests Mia. "Of course!" replies Coppélia. She puts on some music and teaches Mia and Leo a simple dance. It's just for two people, so they all take turns. Suddenly, something in the wardrobe catches Leo's eye. He climbs in to investigate and Mia follows.

The music is fun and loud and jolly,
and it's all about a dancing dolly!

The subtitle of Coppélia is "The Girl with the Enamel Eyes". This is because many old wooden dolls had enamel eyes. Enamel is a type of glass that is often used in jewellery.

The composer of *Coppélia* is Léo Delibes. He wrote short tunes to represent each character. They were played every time that character came on stage, or when the composer wanted to remind you of them.

One, two, three, four, five... dancing makes her come alive!

Coppélia is a funny ballet all about an inventor who makes a very lifelike, full-size doll. In fact, she looks so real that a man named Franz falls in love with her!

"Where are we?" Leo asks Mia. They look around at a field full of bright flowers. Above their heads, windmills make a whooshing sound as their sails spin around. "The Netherlands," replies Mia. "The Netherlands is windy, it's great for a kite, Belgium's below it, and Germany's right!" Leo laughs. He spots a farmer wearing traditional clothes and shoes. Mia points to the farmer's feet excitedly. "Those things on his feet are called clogs, and they're made from wood!" The farmer hops onto a stone and begins to tap and stamp his clogs. "I love his dance!" says Leo. He and Mia decide to join in and give the dance a go themselves.

Set in a field where it's bright and sunny,
this ballet is great and very funny!

A "pas de trois" is a dance performed by three people. It's usually in five sections; one for all three dancers, one solo for each dancer, and then a little section at the end.
La Fille mal gardée is a ballet about Lise and Colas. The pair are in love, but everyone seems to want to keep them apart. In one of the ballet's most famous scenes, they perform a ribbon dance around a maypole.
Here they hop like frogs, push to hear wooden clogs!
The main dancer in the "Clog Dance" is Lise's mother. She is a bit like a pantomime dame! This role is usually given to a dancer that has been a member of the ballet company for a long time.

The Firebird is a magical story about Prince Ivan, an evil magician called Koschei (pronounced CO-SHY), a flaming Firebird, and 13 princesses. When Ivan falls in love with one of the princesses, the Firebird helps Ivan to break Koschei's spell and set the princesses free.

"This is where the river meets the sea," Mia explains. Her and Leo have walked a long way and reached an estuary. All around them, reeds are blowing in the wind. "It looks like they're dancing," says Leo. Suddenly, an enormous flock of birds – too many to count – flies overhead. "The birds are moving in one big shape!" Leo says, pointing. "It's called a murmuration," replies Mia, who learned about them on a family walk. The murmuration quickly changes shape, and now it looks like one huge bird! Leo and Mia try to dance like the giant bird, pretending to have its enormous, fiery wings. "Quick," calls Mia. "We don't want to miss the boat to Granny's!"

A round dance is a dance performed in circles. In "The Round Dance of the Princesses" from *The Firebird*, the princesses move elegantly in many different circles.

Igor Stravinsky composed the music for *The Firebird*. He was so keen that he began writing the music before he was even asked to do it!

"This place is enormous," whispers Leo. Him and Mia find Mia's granny in the attic of her house. She's surrounded by paintings, clothes, old-fashioned records, and a gramophone. "My granny doesn't usually let me come up here," replies Mia. "So who knows what we'll find." Leo picks up one of the records and reads the name on the front: *Swan Lake*. Mia opens a dusty book filled with pictures. "Look at this one. They look so elegant," she says pointing to a photo of ballerinas in white costumes. They're dancing together like a parade of baby swans. "Did you know that baby swans are called cygnets?" asks Leo. "I didn't," replies Mia. "Let's do some really big jumps, Leo... one, two, three, FOUR!"

"Corps de ballet" is the name for the dancers in a ballet company who are not the principal dancers or soloists.

In *Swan Lake*, Prince Siegfried meets a girl called Odette who has been changed into a white swan by an evil spell. The spell can be broken only if someone truly loves Odette. At a party, Siegfried meets Odile who looks just like Odette, but Odile is dressed in all black. Siegfried is tricked into marrying Odile, but by the time he realizes she is not Odette, it is too late.

Pyotr Tchaikovsky is the composer of *Swan Lake*. For a long time in the early 1900s, Tchaikovsky's music was left out of productions of the ballet. Thankfully, his music eventually began to be used again.

Mia and Leo are having so much fun jumping that they almost miss Leo's sister's wedding! Everyone is dressed in their best clothes and fanciest outfits. The bride and groom start to slowly dance in the middle of the floor. "The bride's white dress is really pretty," whispers Mia. "She reminds me a bit of a ballerina." Then, the music changes, and all the bridesmaids start dancing with the bride. Everyone watches as they move perfectly in time. The music gets faster and livelier, and soon, all the guests are dancing too. "If I get married, I'm going to dance down the aisle instead of walking!" laughs Leo. Suddenly, all the fairy lights start to twinkle...

"Adagio" means "very slowly". A "grand adage" is when a ballet dancer performs slow, graceful movements with her partner. However, a *grand adage* isn't always accompanied by *adagio* music!

When *Giselle* was performed at the Mariinsky Theatre in Russia in 1911, a famous ballet dancer called Nijinsky danced in tights. It was the first time this had ever happened, as, at that time, male dancers wore trousers. He was fired!

The ballet *Giselle* is about a country girl who falls in love with a nobleman in disguise called Albrecht. When Giselle finds out who Albrecht really is, she dies of a broken heart and becomes a ghost. She stops her fellow ghosts – who are known as "The Wilis" – from harming Albrecht, and this brings them both peace.

The ballet *Spartacus* is named after the king Spartacus, who has been captured by the Roman soldier Crassus. Crassus has also captured Spartacus's wife, Phrygia. Spartacus is able to escape and set Phrygia free too. But eventually, in a sad ending, the Romans return to defeat Spartacus.

Leo and Mia find themselves inside a majestic arena made of ancient stone called a colosseum. "This is like a football stadium," says Mia, looking for a ball to start a match. "Actually, this was a huge open air theatre where people would gather for all sorts of events like plays and dances," Leo explains. They run to the centre of the colosseum and there, in the round, a performance is taking place. The dancers are swaying and twirling majestically. Mia nudges Leo. "This is a dance from the ballet *Spartacus*. It's set in Roman times," she says, pointing to the dancers' costumes. Mia and Leo decide to join in, taking it in turns being the leader. They tilt and twist until they can no longer make out the walls of the colosseum.

"Renversé" is a French word meaning "upset". This move involves the dancer arching and tilting their back. There are lots of *renversé* movements in *Spartacus*.
The king Spartacus is very brave,
he knows that Phrygia he must save!
Of all the ballets in this book, *Spartacus* is probably the least successful. It is mainly performed in Armenia now, and very little elsewhere.
Push the button from above, to hear the gentle music of love.

The stone walls of the colosseum have disappeared, and in their place are the striped sides of a huge tent. The sweet smell of candyfloss is wafting through the air, and on the far side of the tent, people are watching a puppet show. "This tent is called a big top," says Mia. At that moment, lively music begins to play, and a very bright spotlight points its beam upwards. "Look!" cries Leo, pointing. Mia gasps wide-eyed at two people hanging from small rope swings. Leo and Mia are silent for a while, watching the amazing high-wire routine. "It's like they're dancing... but in midair!" whispers Mia. Leo takes Mia's hand, and they climb onto the rope swings. Soon, they're even higher than the performers.

When ballet dancers are on tiptoes, this is called "en pointe". When dancers are in this position, they wear pointe shoes. These shoes have blocks in the toes and silky outsides. Dancers must be very experienced to wear pointe shoes.

A ballet story with a twist...
... one character does not exist!
***Don Quixote* includes** a character called Dulcinea del Toboso who isn't real. Don Quixote makes her up because he wants people to think he has a companion. Even though she is Don Quixote's invention, there's a statue of her in Madrid!
The ballet *Don Quixote* is about the adventures of the Spanish nobleman Don Quixote and his servant Sancho Panza. The pair seem to cause a fuss wherever they go: at a street carnival in Barcelona; at a puppet show; and even at a wedding.
Press once and you can hear, the dance when matadors appear.

"Wow! Look at the size of this place," gasps Mia. She and Leo are inside an enormous castle in a grand ballroom. "The floor looks very shiny. Maybe I could slide along it?" wonders Leo. Before he can try, Mia grabs his hand. "Let's dance the waltz!" She starts to show Leo the dance her mum taught her. "You do it together and count like this: ONE, two-three, ONE, two-three," instructs Mia. "I'd love to be able to dance *en pointe* one day," says Leo while still counting. "In the ballet *The Sleeping Beauty*, Princess Aurora stays *en pointe* for ages!" It's been a long and exciting day, and Mia and Leo are starting to feel as sleepy as Aurora. It's time to go home!

The Sleeping Beauty ballet is based on the classic fairytale. Aurora is cursed by a wicked fairy. After sleeping for 100 years, she is awoken by a kiss from Prince Désiré. When Aurora and the prince marry, even Puss-in-Boots shows up for the wedding!

When Alexander III – the Emperor of Russia – attended the premiere of *The Sleeping Beauty*, he annoyed Tchaikovsky by giving his verdict: "Very nice." Tchaikovsky was hoping for something more enthusiastic!

Press for a lively tune, perfect for waltzing around the room!

A "grand adage à la rose" is just like a *grand adage*, but this time, Aurora dances with four people, each offering her a rose. She must hold many poses perfectly for a very long time, so this is a real test for the ballet dancer playing Aurora.

Leo and Mia are at their very first ballet lesson together. "This room is amazing!" says Leo. All around are other excited children. Huge mirrors hang along the walls, and in the corner, someone is playing a piano. "Now we can try out all the things we saw on our adventure!" says Mia excitedly. Today is an extra special class, because a group of real ballet dancers have come in dressed in long white skirts. "They're called tutus," says Leo. The ballet dancers teach all the children how to do a *plié* by bending their knees down and then up. "I think I'm going to like this ballet thing!" grins Leo.

The music for *Les Sylphides* is by a composer called Frédéric Chopin. Chopin didn't write the music specifically for the ballet, and it began to be used long after he wrote it.

Les Sylphides doesn't tell a story. Instead, it is a series of dances for a large group of dancers. The dancers represent "sylphides" – spirits dressed in white. All the separate dances are set to the music of Chopin. When it was first staged, this ballet wasn't called *Les Sylphides*. It was called *Chopiniana*, meaning a collection of Chopin pieces.

What's this ballet all about? Press to find out!

"Ballet blanc" is French for "white ballet". It is used to describe ballets in which all the dancers wear white. Often, a *ballet blanc* has no story and is simply a string of beautiful dances.

All in a row and dressed in white,
the dancers are a wonderful sight!

Ballet Positions

That's the end of Leo and Mia's adventures for today, but why not try some moves yourself! There are five basic positions in ballet. In each position, the way you hold your arms or legs – and sometimes both – changes. Remember to stand up straight, and let's get started!

First position

Hold your arms in a circle in front of your body. Keep your legs together and turn them outwards so that your feet look like the letter "V" from above.

Second position

Open your arms out to the side but keep them rounded. Keep your legs turned outwards and move your feet apart.

Third position

Slide your right leg slightly in front of the other so that the back of your heel is against the side of your other foot. Move your right arm above your front foot so that it is in the same place as it was in first position, and keep holding your left arm out to the side.

Fourth position

Lift the arm above your front foot into a rounded position above your head. Keep your legs turned out and slide your front foot forwards so that there is a space between your front and back feet. This position is a little trickier, so take your time!

Fifth position

Raise both of your arms above your head in a rounded position. Cross your front foot across your back foot so that the heel of your front foot is in front of the toes of your back foot.

Meet the composers

Pyotr Ilyich Tchaikovsky
The Nutcracker, Swan Lake, and The Sleeping Beauty

The Russian composer Pyotr Ilyich Tchaikovsky (1840-1893) began writing when he was four years old. He wrote three great ballets, and you can see all of them in this book. He conducted his own music around the world – even though he was scared of performing in public!

Léo Delibes
Coppélia

Léo Delibes (1836-1891) was a French composer of ballets and operas. He studied music at the Conservatoire de Paris where he was taught by Adolphe Adam, the composer of *Giselle*.

Ferdinand Hérold
La Fille mal gardée

Ferdinand Hérold (1791-1833) was a French composer known for composing music for piano, operas, and ballets as well as choral music. He was famous for being one of the first composers to write more complicated pieces that reflected the movements being performed by the ballet dancers.

Igor Stravinsky
The Firebird

The Russian composer Igor Stravinsky's (1882-1971) music was sometimes *so* original and *so* different that many people found it hard to understand. At one of his ballets, the audience was so shocked that a riot broke out!

Adolphe Adam
Giselle

Before he became a successful composer, Frenchman Adolphe Adam (1803-1856) had various other jobs. At one point, he was the triangle player in a Paris theatre band – and he did it without being paid!

Aram Khachaturian
Spartacus

Aram Khachaturian (1903-1978) was a tuba player and self-taught piano player. He had no music lessons until he was 18, when he enrolled at music college. He loved folk music – the native music handed down through the years – of his home country, Armenia. As well as composing music for ballets, he also composed the music for the Armenian national anthem.

Ludwig Minkus
Don Quixote

Ludwig Minkus's (1826-1917) real first name was Aloysius. Although he was a great violin player and a well-known music teacher, he is remembered today for his ballet music. Some say he developed his love of music while helping at his father's restaurant – which had its own orchestra – in Austria.

Frédéric Chopin
Les Sylphides

Frédéric Chopin (1810-1849) was a composer who loved to write for the piano. In fact, not one piece of his music didn't feature a piano... and he wrote more than 150 works! Chopin also enjoyed writing Mazurkas, a traditional dance in his homeland of Poland.

Legendary choreographers and performers

MARIUS PETIPA (1818-1910) was one of the most famous choreographers and was responsible for more than 100 ballets. He was involved in choreographing seven of the ballets in this book: *Coppélia*, *Don Quixote*, *Giselle*, *La Fille mal gardée*, *Swan Lake*, *The Nutcracker*, and *The Sleeping Beauty*. Phew!

The original choreographer of *Coppélia* was ARTHUR SAINT-LÉON (1821-1870). He also invented a way of writing down choreography, including the movement of the feet, arms, head, and body. As a result, the dance steps could be recreated.

FREDERICK ASHTON (1904-1988) was the chief choreographer with the Royal Ballet. Ashton is often said to have created the English style of ballet. In this style of ballet, the upper body stays quite still, and the movements are very elegant.

MIKHAIL FOKINE (1880-1942) was a legendary Russian choreographer. After success with both the Russian Imperial Ballet and the Ballets Russes, he moved to America. There, he founded the American Ballet Company. He was also a great painter and played the Russian mandolin called a balalaika.

Marius Petipa was not the only choreographer of *Swan Lake*. LEV IVANOV (1834-1901) choreographed the second and fourth acts of the ballet. Both of Ivanov's sections feature lots of swans dressed in flowing white, and so these are often called "the white acts".

JEAN CORALLI (1779-1854) and JULES PERROT (1810-1892) were both dancers who became choreographers. Together, they choreographed *Giselle* at the Paris Opéra. However, Coralli is the only one credited with this, as Perrot was not employed by the Paris Opéra, and so they overlooked his contribution.

Although LEONID YAKOBSON (1904-1975) choreographed the original dance moves to *Spartacus*, not everyone liked his steps. Some wanted more ballet *en pointe*, so the later choreography by YURI GRIGOROVICH (1927-present) has become more famous.

ANNA PAVLOVA (1881-1931) was one of the most famous ballet dancers ever. She was a principal dancer with the Imperial Russian Ballet and Ballets Russes. She left to form her own ballet company and was the first ballerina to tour the world performing.

MIKHAIL BARYSHNIKOV (1948-present) is often called the world's greatest living male ballet dancer. He has starred in ballets around the world and in several films. While female dancers are sometimes called ballerinas, male dancers are called "danseurs".

MISTY COPELAND (1982-present) was promoted to principal dancer with the American Ballet Theatre in 2015. She is the first Black woman in the ballet company's history to hold the position. Misty did not start ballet until she was 13 years old.

Did you spot the mouse?

Did you spot Matilda the mouse hiding on the pages of this book? If so, well done! If you didn't, why not look again now – she appears 10 times.

Answers: **p. 2** Under the window, behind the presents. **p. 5** Behind the leg of the bed. **p. 6** Among the tulips to the left of Leo and Mia. **p. 9** Among the grass. **p. 10** Behind the telephone. **p. 12** Under the cake table. **p. 15** On the top wall of the coliseum. **p. 16** To the left of the puppet show. **p. 18** Behind the ginger-haired man. **p. 21** Behind the piano.

Acknowledgements

Published by Dorling Kindersley Ltd in association with Classic FM, part of Global Media and Entertainment Group Ltd.

Coppélia, Don Quixote, Giselle, Swan Lake, The Nutcracker, and *The Sleeping Beauty* licensed courtesy of Naxos Music UK Limited.

Les Sylphides licensed courtesy of Capriccio.

La Fille mal gardée licensed courtesy of Warner Music UK Limited.

Spartacus and *The Firebird* licensed courtesy of Onyx Classics Ltd.

Sounds edited by James Brady

Editor Vicky Armstrong
Senior Designer Clive Savage
Production Editor Siu Yin Chan
Senior Production Controller Louise Daly
Senior Acquisitions Editor Katy Flint
Managing Art Editor Vicky Short
Publishing Director Mark Searle

First published in Great Britain in 2023 by Dorling Kindersley Limited
DK, One Embassy Gardens, 8 Viaduct Gardens, London SW11 7BW

The authorised representative in the EEA is Dorling Kindersley Verlag GmbH. Arnulfstr. 124, 80636 Munich, Germany.

10 9 8 7 6 5 4 3 2 1
001–334896–October/2023

A CIP catalogue record for this book is available from the British Library.
ISBN: 978-0-2416-1199-9

Printed and bound in China

For the curious
www.dk.com

This book was made with Forest Stewardship Council™ certified paper – one small step in DK's commitment to a sustainable future.
For more information go to www.dk.com/our-green-pledge